Outst
Leade

Fast Track to Business Excellence

Other books in the series:

Exceptional Entrepreneurship

Managing Your People

Mastering Change

Fast Track to Business Excellence

Outstanding Leadership

Real-Life Lessons from Top Business Leaders

Adapted from the Fifty Lessons
management collection

Published by BBC Books,
BBC Worldwide Limited,
Woodlands, 80 Wood Lane,
London W12 0TT

First published 2005
Copyright © Fifty Lessons, 2005

ISBN: 0563 51938 X

Commissioning Editor
Emma Shackleton
Editors for Fifty Lessons
Adam Sodowick and **Jenny Watts**
Editor
Sarah Sutton
Designer
Andrew Barron @ Thextension
Typesetter
Kevin O'Connor
Production Controller
Man Fai Lau

Set in Clarendon Light and Scala sans
Printed and bound in Great Britain by
Goodman Baylis

Contents

Acknowledgements

We would like to thank all of the executives who have contributed their hard-won lessons to the Fifty Lessons business library.

We believe that recording the first-hand learning experiences of today's business leaders will prove to be of immeasurable value to the business leaders of the future.

We'd also like to thank all those who have believed in, and contributed their time to, this growing and exciting initiative. Your support has been invaluable.

From the team at Fifty Lessons

About Fifty Lessons

Wherever you are on the career ladder, you are walking in the footsteps of others. Whatever business dilemma you are facing, some of the finest brains in business have faced it before.

Fifty Lessons was born out of a desire to learn from the experience of today's greatest business minds. We felt that decades of hard-won business experience were being written off to the vagaries of memory and resolved to capture, store and pass on this wisdom to the next generation.

Using the power of storytelling, we have captured on film the most valuable and defining experiences of some of the biggest names in international business, and built them into a digital library containing over 400 lessons.

The *Fast Track to Business Excellence* series features specially chosen lessons from this library, offering inspiration, practical help and guidance across a diverse range of management challenges. In business, as in life, learning from the knowledge of others is invaluable. We believe that there is no substitute for experience.

Adam Sodowick
Co-founder

For access to filmed interviews from the entire Fifty Lessons management collection, please visit: www.fiftylessons.com

Introduction to Outstanding Leadership

An outstanding business needs to encourage outstanding leadership. With it comes effective communication, improved performance and business growth. Without it an organization will drift or fracture, allowing the competition to gain the advantage.

Outstanding Leadership gives you access to the real-life business experience of twelve exceptional business leaders in a pocket-sized format. Their personal stories, and how they learnt from their experiences, provide winning strategies and a fast track to understanding the best approaches to leadership.

The book begins with the need to take responsibility for the actions of the organization, to eliminate a blame culture, and to set clear goals for people to buy into and follow. Core characteristics of leadership include a talent for perseverance, a willingness to be visible and to lead from the front, and having the courage of your convictions. The book ends on the importance of understanding and appreciating the value of people and their expertise. True leadership ability is a rare asset and it should be nurtured at all costs.

Whatever your level of management experience, these personal stories provide invaluable knowledge, insight and understanding of how best to be an outstanding leader.

> Responsibility lies ultimately with the company's Chief Executive. Being in charge means just that; people should not blame subordinates or try to pass the buck.

1a

Eliminate Blame
Domenico De Sole

Director, *Procter & Gamble*; former President & CEO, *Gucci Group*

My Career

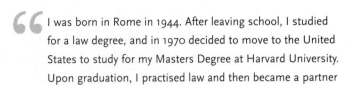

I was born in Rome in 1944. After leaving school, I studied for a law degree, and in 1970 decided to move to the United States to study for my Masters Degree at Harvard University. Upon graduation, I practised law and then became a partner in the Washington law firm of Patton, Boggs & Blow.

My career at Gucci began in 1984, when I joined the company as Chief Executive Officer of Gucci America. I remained in New York until 1994, but then moved to Italy to take up my role as the Group's Chief Operating Officer. I was appointed President and CEO of Gucci Group NV the following year, and became Chairman of the Group's Management Board.

During this time I worked hard to re-establish the exclusivity and profitability of the Gucci brand, which we achieved by focusing on Gucci's core leather products and investing in advertising and communication, as well as in men's clothing and women's ready-to-wear fashion. Important elements of this strategy included the strengthening of the company's information and logistics processes, improving efficiency, and upgrading and expanding the network of directly operated stores.

At the end of 1995 Gucci Group NV was listed on the New York and Amsterdam stock exchanges. This was followed in 1997 by the purchase of Gucci's Timepieces, the company's most important licence. In 1999 we successfully fought a hostile takeover bid, and the outcome further enhanced shareholder value. In the same year we also began a new phase of acquisition: Gucci completed the purchase of Yves Saint Laurent, Sanofi Beauté (now YSL Beauté) and Sergio Rossi; in 2000 we acquired Boucheron, Alexander McQueen and Bedat & Co, and in 2001 Bottega Veneta, Stella McCartney and Balenciaga SA, owner of the Balenciaga luxury brand.

One of the most pleasing outcomes for me is that during my time leading the Gucci Group we went from bankruptcy in 1994 to being the third largest – and one of the most profitable – luxury multi-brand companies in the world. At the end of April 2004 the Gucci Group's largest shareholder, the French retail group Pinault Printemps Redoute, took complete control. I retired from my role within Gucci soon afterwards, and I am now a Director of Procter & Gamble, as well as a Director of Gap Inc, Bausch & Lomb, and Telecom Italia.

Domenico De Sole

Director, *Procter & Gamble*; former President & CEO, *Gucci Group*

Eliminate Blame

The manager or the CEO is always responsible. This great principle is incredibly important for good management. I remember that Maurizio Gucci, the former CEO and the last family member to manage the company, was always critical of his organization. The thing that struck me as really bizarre was that he was always blaming somebody else for its problems. If a collection was not very good, he would blame his designer; then he would complain about stores not displaying the collection on time, being late, or pricing too expensively. Then he would blame the creative director who developed the store. We were talking about it one day and finally I said, 'But Maurizio, you are the CEO – you run the company. How can you blame everybody else for everything that goes wrong in the company? You are in charge. You are responsible. If you don't think these people know what they are doing, you should fire them – but if they are there because you trust and value them, then it's up to you to make sure that they execute their responsibilities properly.'

Unfortunately, I see this habit in a lot of companies. People try to blame subordinates. I think blaming subordinates is silly. Either you're in charge or you're not in charge. If you are the person who makes the final decisions, and you are the person who appoints the other people, then in the end you are responsible. I always say jokingly that in my company if the fashion show is great, the designer takes all the credit. If the fashion show is bad, it's my fault. At the end he – and everybody else – reports to me, so the CEO must take responsibility.

Typically, CEOs who are not very good will always look for who did it.

I really think the best thing you learn in business is that you make mistakes. Everybody makes mistakes, and the people in charge must be in charge and take responsibility for failure, even taking responsibility for the failure to supervise somebody else – so there really is no excuse. Typically, CEOs who are not very good will always look for who did it. They will try to find a culprit. I really do believe that that is irrelevant. If a mistake has been made, the responsibility must be assumed at the management level, then the situation should be moved forward to understand *why* the mistake was made in order to avoid the same mistake being made twice.

I have never blamed anybody else in my life, but the corollary of this is that I do expect performance from people. I need them to understand that if they're in charge, they're in charge. They are responsible for producing the results and for making sure that everything gets done properly.

The senior management sets the culture and tone of an organization. It should lead by example, and through personal commitment energize the team and ensure that everyone understands and responds to the identified goals.

1b   The CEO Sets the Tone

A mission statement should be clear and repeated regularly.

It is totally clear to me that any company wanting to be successful must have a very precise sense of its mission: it must know where it is going and how it plans to get from A to B. Most importantly, the manager must set the tone of the mission. That is critical. Each layer of management, whether at senior or middle level, needs to understand what the mission is, what the company is trying to achieve, and what the goals of the company are. These goals must be very clear, simple and expressed in a way that makes them easily understood. What I say to everybody is that a mission statement should be clear and repeated regularly.

It is important for a CEO to keep repeating the same basic principle in order to make sure that everybody at every level of the organization commits to the mission, shares the dream and understands what needs to be done. By the same token, I am a true believer that senior management must set the tone, and that begins with the CEO. For example, it is very difficult to say to people that they have to save money if there is a management style in place that is wasteful. That is true for everything. It's difficult to create a culture of hard work and responsibility if there is no culture of hard work at the CEO level.

When I went to Italy back in 1993 or 1994 my immediate priority was to get everybody in agreement about the internal mission, to understand what we were trying to do and to start executing it properly. I used to be there all the time. I would arrive at the crack of dawn and still be there very late every night; I would work on weekends, and I would call people all the time and at any time. When I said that something needed to be done, I would keep following up and calling back, asking: 'Has it been done?' I was very visible. I was living in Florence at the time and visiting all our suppliers in the area, so I had a very strong presence within the organization and made sure that everybody communicated with me; but, importantly, I also used to communicate with them. At that time I had more people reporting to me and the company was smaller, but the sense that things were going to change and that things needed to be done was very strong. They saw me working full time.

Luxury companies are very strong in Asia, so I started travelling there too – constantly – because I recognized that this was an important market for us to grow. Again, I established a very strong presence and demonstrated to a lot of people that there was very strong personal commitment on my part.

I really do feel that one of the most important tenets for a CEO or a manager is to make sure that everybody views you as a person who practises what he preaches. You have to set the tone, be the leader and set the example. Second, it is important that the mission is stated simply, clearly and repeated at regular intervals to make sure that it filters through the entire organization, and everybody really understands the goal of the company, what it is trying to achieve and how to get there. **„**

Executive Timeline Domenico De Sole

1970	Moved from Italy to the USA.
Early years	Masters Degree – Harvard University
	Patton, Boggs & Blow
	Partner
	Patton, Boggs & Blow is a Washington law firm.
1984	**Gucci**
	Joined what has become one of the world's leading multi-brand companies in the luxury goods market.
1984–1994	**Gucci America Inc**
	Chief Executive Officer
1994	**Gucci Group NV**
	Group Chief Operating Officer
	Moved to Italy.
1995	Led Gucci Group NV's listing on the New York and Amsterdam stock exchanges.
1999	Successfully fought a hostile takeover bid, securing Gucci's independence as a basis for continued expansion, including the acquisition of Yves Saint Laurent, Alexander McQueen and Stella McCartney.
1995–2004	*President and Chief Executive Officer*
2004–present	**Procter & Gamble**, Cincinnati
	Director
	P&G is a leading manufacturer of consumer health and beauty products.

Every leader has a responsibility to set the right tone at the top. To live the values the company espouses and to lead by example; just repeating the rhetoric is not enough.

2a   **Setting the Right Tone at the Top**
Michael Rake

Chairman, *KPMG International*

My Career

My career has been interesting. I became an accountant very reluctantly at a time when I decided the UK was going down the drain. I wanted to qualify and leave the country, and thought the best way to do this was to become a Chartered Accountant. I qualified in the UK, then left immediately for Belgium with the firm I was articled to at the time. I spent the next fourteen years in Continental Europe, and ended up running their audit business in Belgium and Luxembourg. I transferred in 1974 to what was then Peat Marwick. I moved to run the Middle East practice from 1986 to 1989, before briefly running the Belgium practice, and then returning to the UK to become a Board Member. I had various major international clients and held various management positions within the UK. I was elected UK Senior Partner in 1998, European Chairman in 1999, and Global Chairman in 2002.

Michael Rake

Chairman, *KPMG International*

The tone that an individual leader sets is the most important in influencing the way that the organization works as a whole.

In the past few years a complete breakdown in trust has developed in the business world. There has been a breakdown in trust in the operation of the capital markets, in the trust of chief executives and the way they operate, and there is an assumption that everyone operates out of a sense of greed, if not dishonesty, enriching themselves at the expense of others. This is one of the results of the impact of recent corporate scandals not only in the United States, but also in the UK. As a consequence, we've seen the evolution of an enormous amount of regulation, legislation, litigation and rule-making. Yet, for me, the reason we've had these problems and these cases of extreme behaviour and extreme greed relates to the underlying culture of an organization.

Things can go wrong from operational and environmental points of view, but if you examine corporate culture, you often find that it's the tone at the top, the tone that an individual leader sets, that is most important in influencing the way an organization works as a whole. We need to understand the importance of this issue when we take responsibility for public companies, whether as advisers, auditors, or as Non-executive Directors, because if the leadership doesn't set the right tone, it's amazing how even intelligent people become overwhelmed by the prevailing culture. That was clearly the case in Enron, and has clearly been the case in many other companies where the culture went wrong at the top.

This introduces the real issue of leadership by example, because one of the key things leaders have to understand is that they're extremely visible. Anything they do is exaggerated when communicated across the company, so their attitude towards life, their basic values and what they say are very important. How do managers behave towards other people? Do they have a sense of integrity? What degree of respect do they hold for other people within the organization, whatever their level, and is it genuine respect rather than paying lip-service to a charter? Enron had a laudable charter of values in Corporate Social Responsibility (CSR), but underneath it was almost a smokescreen for abuse.

Organizations need a corporate culture where people can see that the values go beyond rhetoric, beyond a charter of values, and that the ethos is sincere – people at the top really live the values of the organization. The reason companies endorse concepts like CSR is that they are incredibly important to the corporate reputation; such concepts are not only the right thing for the communities that businesses operate within, but the business case is enormously important too. CSR enables a company to portray a positive image to the outside world. It adds value to its brand, it adds prestige and pride to its people, it aids recruitment and retention, and it also creates the right culture within a capitalist world.

Capitalism and public companies: the only reason we have them is so that they create wealth for many rather than just a few. For that premise to be trusted, and to be seen and believed in by employees, regulators, politicians and journalists, the company has to act upon its principles: it has to deliver and live by them. In my experience, for this to work it always begins by the person at the top setting the example.

What is striking in investigations that KPMG has done into companies and individuals where things have gone wrong is that often we find that the individuals involved don't realize that they have committed an illegal act. They have crossed the line, if you like, from white to grey to black. Where the organizational culture has gone wrong, or the tone at the top is wrong, most of them have had to operate within the grey area for a lot of the time. Therefore, when they cross into the black area and actually commit an illegal and criminal act, they don't realize that they have crossed that line. When you interview these individuals you find that because the culture of the organization has gone wrong, and because of the aggressiveness with which the targets are set, or the ways in which their achievement of those targets is rewarded, intelligent and innately honest people suddenly think that their actions are acceptable, because within that environment they seem to be okay. However they are not okay, and they've done something that is illegal, immoral or criminal.

Organizations and leaders need to create an environment that actually rewards the right culture. People who are promoted

W here the organizational culture has gone wrong, people have had to operate within a grey area … when they commit a criminal act, they don't realize they have crossed a line.

into management roles need to be role models and seen to be people who demonstrate corporate values and integrity of approach. People who have been properly counselled or advised and who still do not adopt the corporate values need to be dealt with. However clever or technically brilliant they might be, if they're creating an environment where the culture is wrong, they're going to be a net deficit to the organization. Management needs to think seriously about removing them, because such behaviour is pernicious, and destructive attitudes can spread, creating an environment where people think that you have to behave in an inappropriate way in order to survive or succeed. It's very damaging for an organization. Not every case ends like Enron, but in a lot of companies that fail or become inefficient due to an unhealthy corporate culture, the people have become demotivated. In a large organization you have to work very hard to ensure that people understand the corporate values and the way they as individuals should operate.

The basic lesson is that it is the responsibility of any leader to set the right tone at the top, to live the values that the company espouses and to lead by example.

Learn to be self-reliant and resilient from a young age; there will always be unexpected issues to face, and as a leader you need continuously to project confidence so that your people trust in your ability to find the solution.

2b   **The Self-reliant Leader**

The Self-reliant Leader

I was fortunate in that I learnt how to be self-reliant and resilient very early on in my management experience. It is critically important to learn these skills young, otherwise, when you reach the top of an organization, particularly a large one, you may find yourself in quite a lonely position. When you are at the top you need continuously to project confidence, you need to reflect something that your people understand and have confidence in.

For me, learning these lessons goes back to 1986, when I was asked by KPMG to go to the Middle East. It was the time of the Iran/Iraq war and there were huge financial crises occurring in the banking sector in the region. We had a lot of difficulties in our business there: two or three of our people were under investigation by the judicial authorities; we didn't have enough cash to pay the wages at the end of the month; and, I think the day after I'd been told that, we lost a client that was worth about 30 per cent of our revenues. I remember calling my boss in London to let him know and he said: 'Well, good luck, Mike!' It was a very good lesson for me.

We went from near collapse and catastrophe to assembling a group of people who realized we had to deal with the situation. We not only dealt with the immediate issues, but also within the next very difficult two years we recovered our market position, were highly profitable, were remitting profits back to the head office, and people were willing and keen to join us. Our reputation had been fully re-established.

One needed to be pretty tough in confronting the situation, recognizing that one had no choice but to get on with it, to ensure that people had some confidence – even though I wasn't quite sure what on earth I was going to do to resolve matters. I think the fact that people had confidence meant that the team really pulled together. There was a realization that together we *had* to find a solution because no one was going to help us, so we might as well get out there and do something about it. That gave us the impetus to fight back.

It appeared at the beginning that everything was against us, but step by step we dealt with one thing, then another, then another; and we found that if we worked hard enough at it, we suddenly got a bit of good luck too, and events started to go in the right direction. Learning to deal with each and every issue, learning that there is no escape but to deal with them yourself, realizing that you have to motivate people to work with you to find solutions, and being absolutely determined because you have no choice, are enormously important lessons. The younger you learn them, the better for you.

It comes down to understanding how an individual and an organization interrelate. If people understand that, they will be given some authority with responsibility. People need to understand that if they make a decision and it's the right one, they will get credit for it, but what they will never be allowed to do is make no decision and pass it to somebody else.

Step by step we dealt with one thing, then another, then another; and we found that if we worked hard enough at it, we suddenly got a bit of good luck too, and events started to go in the right direction.

There are some people in senior positions who love to make all the decisions, so to some extent they create an environment of dependence. Whilst they must be resilient and self-reliant, leaders should not plan or expect to make every decision, because if they do, the result will be that every decision is pushed in their direction for them to make, and no one else in the organization will make decisions. There will be sclerosis of the organization, stemming from the top, because everything has to come from one person. This situation needs to be avoided. It's characteristic of what you'd call a 'control freak' in a command-and-control environment. In an empowered environment, where people can deal with issues, they will come up with solutions and implement them, knowing they won't always get it right, but knowing they're expected to do something to make a difference, and to deal with the issues they face.

When in a leadership position, it is important to ensure that the people whom you are developing within the organization are given the opportunity to gain experience where they have to be self-reliant and learn to handle issues. Everybody knows, in whatever business they are in – whether running a medical practice, an accounting practice, or a FTSE 100 company – that there are times when you get bad news and things go wrong. Learning to deal with bad news is critical, as is the ability to turn it round, and ask: 'What can I do?', 'What are the good things?' and 'What are the silver linings within that particular cloud?'

P eople need to understand that if they make a decision and it's the right one, they will get credit for it, but what they will never be allowed to do is make no decision and pass it to somebody else.

How you react to each situation is critically important to the people around you, to how the organization sees you, and therefore to how the organization responds to that particular crisis. If you start getting downcast or depressed, you will have grave difficulty in bringing your people with you. 99

1972	Qualified in accountancy in London
1974	**KPMG (Peat Marwick)**
1984–1986	Ran audit businesses in Belgium and Luxembourg
1986–1989	**KPMG Middle East**
1989	**KPMG (UK)**
	Returned to London
1991	*Member of the UK Board*
1998	*UK Chairman and Senior Partner*
1999	**KPMG (EMEA)**
	Chairman
2002–present	**KPMG International**
	Chairman

Companies must respond to competition and change by deciding how best to use their resources to achieve their overall goals. Chief Executives lead the process by setting a clear, achievable strategy that the management team must then execute

Setting Clear and Achievable Goals

Roger Parry

Chief Executive, *Clear Channel International*

My Career

My business career did not begin in business at all. I was a journalist for quite a long time, working for BBC and Independent Television, covering a whole range of topics, but towards the end of my journalistic career I was focusing on business issues. As a result, I was noticed by McKinsey & Company, the consulting firm. They recruited both myself and a business journalist from the *Financial Times* to join them as consultants. It was a real transition for me as I moved from being someone who made my living out of writing and broadcasting to someone who made my living out of problem solving, because consulting is all about problem solving.

I found that, having got a taste for business via the consulting environment, I wanted very quickly to move into business in a practical way. That's when I went into advertising with a company called WCRS. It then turned into another advertising business called Aegis, which was all about media buying. I have been quite fortunate along the way to have had some entrepreneurial roles: buying and selling a radio station; getting involved in buying into another advertising business, which I then sold on to an American media group. And that's how I ended up where I am now – running Clear Channel. I also hold non-executive roles as Chairman of a newspaper company, and Chairman of a magazine group. It is an extremely satisfying experience to sit as a Non-executive Chairman because you can observe the activities of a Chief Executive without having to carry their responsibilities.

Roger Parry

Chief Executive, *Clear Channel International*

${\rm T}$o make decisions about future direction a Chief Executive needs to have a really thorough understanding of the issues facing the business, and of the environment within which it's operating.

When a Chief Executive sets goals he is really asking questions and making decisions about forward strategy before letting the management tier know what's expected of them. To make decisions about future direction a Chief Executive needs to have a really thorough understanding of the issues facing the business, and of the environment within which it's operating. Only as a consequence of having an understanding of that business environment can a Chief Executive set meaningful goals.

For example, if you have, as I do, a business that operates in more than fifty countries, it doesn't necessarily follow that each General Manager will share exactly the same goal. In China there is an enormous opportunity for growth, so the goal for the General Manager running our Chinese business unit is to look for new investments and ways of putting money to work. At the other end of the extreme is Switzerland, where the market is completely mature. The goal for the General Manager there is to operate at optimum efficiency;

he is looking to do the same amount of business in a more effective way, whereas his Chinese counterpart is simply looking to do more business.

Another important consideration is 'do-ability' – a word that I don't think appears in any English dictionary. By that I mean: 'Is a goal actually achievable?' One of the worst things a CEO can say to an Operating Manager is: 'Here is your goal,' if the Operating Manager's response is: 'Such a thing is impossible.' We are all familiar with how that feels. If you say to a child: 'I want you to jump over a 10-metre hurdle,' the child knows that he can't do it, and will become very upset. In the same way, if you set business goals that are wholly unachievable, the net result will be very disappointed managers and a general feeling of failure.

Some years ago I was working within an advertising agency group where I was responsible for one of the public relations businesses that we had recently acquired. The Chief Executive told us that he wanted this business to double its sales within two years. Now the problem with aiming to double your sales within two years in a business like that is that you have to hire people to do the work. The constraint in this case wasn't winning new clients; the constraint was hiring people because at the time there was a great shortage of them. We walked away from that annual budget review knowing in advance that we were going to fail because it wasn't going to be possible to hire a sufficient number of people, or hire them quickly enough. The same goal – 'double your sales' – had been set for all the businesses across the whole group. We were stuck with something we couldn't possibly achieve and within a short period of time a lot of people were working with a sense of failure. The error was in the original process of setting the goal; everyone had to admit to that, and everyone had to be realistic about it.

When things go wrong it is important to review the problem, otherwise members of staff will become disaffected and the whole organization will become dysfunctional. It is very important that people have goals that are achievable so that they work with a sense of success. That does not mean setting goals that are so easy that everyone achieves them; it is not like following an examination process where everybody passes. The important thing is that if a goal is missed, it is missed for reasons that everyone understands and that can genuinely be put down to *force majeure*. A goal should not be missed because it was so unrealistic that it couldn't be achieved.

Clear goals are established as a result of really understanding the environment within which the business is operating, and also as a result of constructive dialogue between Business Managers and the Chief Executive. Appropriate goals are goals that all parties understand and buy into, rather than being unrealistic figures that are geared to impress shareholders.

It is a Chief Executive's responsibility to make sure that mergers and acquisitions really work. They must know how to get transactions done effectively, how to manage the integration process afterwards, and how to communicate this to stakeholders – both internally and externally.

Making Deals Work

Success or failure of an acquisition or a merger has to be down to the Chief Executive.

There's a real danger from a Chief Executive's point of view that during merger and acquisition transactions, the deal becomes the objective in itself, and people forget about what happens next, after the deal is done. The conventional wisdom is that success has been achieved when the champagne corks pop in the investment bank meeting room, when of course it hasn't. All you've actually done at that stage is bought something or merged with something. The challenge then is to make that acquisition or merger work. This is a responsibility that it's impossible for a Chief Executive to wriggle out of. If you are running a large business, you can sometimes say with legitimacy that you've devolved a lot of the responsibility to the Business Unit Managers and that success or failure within a business unit is down to them, but success or failure of an acquisition or a merger has to be down to the Chief Executive. That CEO is likely to have been the architect of that deal and should be deeply immersed in the issues relating to the transaction.

The first 100 days after the deal is done are the period during which the total focus should be upon making sure that the objectives of the merger or acquisition are clear and achievable. It's at that stage of a corporate marriage or acquisition that people are most confused, worried and in need of very clear direction. I've witnessed on a number of occasions the terrible sense of confusion that occurs during the first two or three months. There can be confusion regarding who is in charge and what the politics are, and there is a sense that in the higher echelons of management people are circling each other, jostling for position. It's an extremely damaging and debilitating period in the life of a business, and it is the role of the Chief Executive to stop the confusion. The answer is to take very early, very quick decisions regarding who is in charge, and if an office is to be closed, it should be announced quickly and closed down quickly to remove the uncertainty.

The issue of managing the transaction itself is easy. There are hundreds of investment bankers and lawyers who will manage the transaction for you, but the moment the deal is done they will vanish; they've all gone and you're left with the results. That's when a good Chief Executive comes into his or her own.

To make a merger or an acquisition successful you have to get as many people as you possibly can to buy into the logic of why the deal has been done in the first place. You have to communicate – you have to over-communicate – to make sure that people really understand what it's all about. It is the role of the Chief Executive at that point to become both visible and voluble in order to sell to everybody the reason a particular deal is being done. If you simply put out a five-line memo that says: 'We've done this deal,' you are not going to bring many people with you. You need to explain that the deal has been done because it will improve the product or it will make the service better or it will make the working conditions better. Emphasize the positives, explain why it has happened and make sure you tell everybody. There is an awful lot of communication required. It is a time when a Chief Executive should be highly visible, very active, and should be talking, writing notes and so on.

In a period of more steady growth Chief Executives should be more distant, but just after a merger or acquisition they need to champion their success, and go out and sell it to all the staff of *both* companies. It's a mistake to assume that because company A buys company B, the people in company A are not destabilized. In reality a good deal combines two businesses, so the people in the originating business may feel just as threatened as the people in the business that has been bought. The Chief Executive needs to sit down with all the managers from both businesses, the two that were merged or the two involved in the acquisition, to listen to them and understand their objectives. However, you can't spend too much time on it; you've got to do it in weeks rather than months. Then you need to tell them that you want them to create a single unified entity. That is the difficult bit because there will inevitably be conflict, and most of us don't really like that.

You are bound to have a situation where two people are doing the same job, and at the end of the day you can keep only one of them. Don't just leave the situation to resolve itself because it never will. It is a very difficult and unpleasant thing to have to say to someone who may be perfectly talented and skilled: 'I'm sorry but there are two of you here and you're the one who is going to go,' but if you take the decision early on you will be doing everyone a favour.

Making the deal work depends on telling everyone why you think the deal is a good idea and communicating how the process is going bring the two organizations together.

Executive Timeline Roger Parry

Early career	*Journalist*
	Seven years working for BBC, commercial TV and radio.
	McKinsey & Company
	Three years with the international firm of management consultants.
	WCRS
	An advertising business.
	Aegis Group
	Development Director
	Aegis is a global media planning and buying company.
1992	Was part of the team that managed the successful restructuring and refinancing of Aegis.
1995–1998	**More Group**
	Chief Executive
	A UK media company acquired by Clear Channel in 1998.
June 1998–present	**Clear Channel International**
	Chief Executive
	Responsible for Clear Channel's operations in Europe, Asia/Pacific and Africa. The company is a world leader in out-of-home media.
2001–present	**Johnston Press**
	Non-executive Chairman
	A UK regional newspaper group.

To encourage your people to achieve the unexpected you need to give them room to breathe and the encouragement to drive and persevere – regardless of perceived odds and hurdles. By being given this chance to grow they can achieve some extraordinary things.

4

Persevere and Achieve the Unexpected
Amelia Fawcett

Vice Chairman, *Morgan Stanley International*

My Career

 I have had an interesting career and one that is not particularly traditional for an investment banker. After university I worked in New York as a paralegal because I had always wanted to be a lawyer – and, indeed, I did become a lawyer. I went to law school at the University of Virginia, and upon graduation moved to New York in the early 1980s to work at a major New York firm, Sullivan & Cromwell. There I focused mainly on banking, mergers and acquisitions and underwriting work. It was a very interesting time to be in New York – the beginning of the era of large international deals, large mergers and acquisitions transactions, and the growth of the financial services business generally.

Towards the end of 1985, Sullivan & Cromwell asked me to go and work in the firm's Paris office. I was very 'disappointed', since I really wanted to live and work in London. However, I was told that, since I spoke French, I was going to go to Paris. After the vibrancy and fast pace of New York, it was a very different place to be – there was not much going on in Financial Services, little public mergers and acquisitions work (much less 'hostile' deals) and the financial markets were rather sleepy – so very different from the Paris financial markets of today! I wondered what I was doing there, but in the end it was a great experience because I did so many different things.

I moved to Morgan Stanley in early 1987 to help set up a Legal and Compliance department. In the early days I focused very much on investment banking, mergers and acquisitions. I advised on the legal and operational sides of deals but gradually began doing more work on the sales and trading side (including derivatives and commodities), as well as being part of the team that opened offices in many countries. I think I have worked (in some capacity) on the opening or establishment of almost every Morgan Stanley office outside the United States, with the exception of Tokyo and Hong Kong. The experience allowed me to work with a variety of people who were building new businesses and looking for people who could help them 'execute' on business plans. So I was asked to come out of the legal department and work for the joint CEOs.

My Europe-wide remit was to work on 1) helping build businesses with governments, as well as policy initiatives with governments, 2) developing a media and communications strategy, and 3) developing community/CSR strategy led by senior management and 4) – as the firm really began to focus on strategic initiatives – to set up a strategy function, then an operational risk function.

I became Chief Administrative Officer and Managing Director in 1996 and Vice Chairman of Morgan Stanley in 2002. In addition I have done a lot of work, which I very much enjoy, outside the firm. Until recently, I was Deputy Chairman of the National Employment Panel. Now I am a member of the Court of the Bank of England, a trustee of the National Portrait Gallery, the Chairman of the London International Festival Theatre, a member of the Governing Council of the University of London and a Trustee of the National Maritime Museum (Cornwall), to name a few.

Amelia Fawcett

Vice Chairman, *Morgan Stanley International*

Persevere and Achieve the Unexpected

I have been impressed over a very long time, both from personal experience and from business experience, at how important perseverance is in achieving the unexpected. I suppose it goes back to being a small child. My grandfather's sister, Aunt Rebecca, used to say to me when I had been particularly difficult: 'Amelia, remember to put your best foot forward...' and I would think: 'Yeah, yeah, yeah...I've heard that before,' but then would come the 'kicker' as she said sternly: 'and keep it there!' That concept of constantly striving and persevering is a lesson well learned as a child. I'd use it even in fishing. You look for a fish and you can't find it or you lose it after presenting a perfect fly to it and then you fish the river for the rest of the day. But in the back of your mind is the recurring thought: 'No, dammit, I'm not going to lose that fish...' So you go back, with a different approach and a different fly, and, sure enough, you land the largest fish of the day.

More recently, the importance of this approach became very clear to me at Morgan Stanley – a large, international financial services firm where technology and systems are global. The perceived wisdom always had been that for a firm to be efficient, solutions *had* to be global, but global solutions can be time-consuming. In an era when we really needed to be more innovative and cost-effective, it seemed odd to me that we couldn't find a way, on a regional basis, to make the business more effective and efficient, even if it was part of a global whole. I wasn't willing to take the view that there was nothing we could do in Europe to improve

'Put your best foot forward...and keep it there.'

and, in doing so, help the global business overall. With all the talented individuals we had, we should have been able to find a solution to take the business – and particularly the operational side of the business – to a different level.

I brought together the top forty people from the infrastructure side of the business. They had varying expertise and were from varying backgrounds: everything from finance to operations to technology. I took them off site (away from the office) and divided them into four groups of ten. I gave each group two days to come up with a business plan for a new business that they would put to venture capitalists (i.e., me and a few other senior managers) to bid for $50 million of investment.

Interestingly, at the end of the two days, every single group came back with the same operational matrix; namely, in order to get a business started and keep it efficient and cost-effective, they would use alternative sourcing, joint ventures or outsourcing. That begged the question for me, and I think for the whole group: 'Why don't we do this back at the office? What's different here?' I then pushed for a group of senior managers to take time away from their day jobs, over a period of several weeks, to analyse all the businesses, all the processes in Europe (line by line), with a view to finding out whether there was a way we could change the paradigm and our working model.

Sure enough, at the end of the process, they came back with a variety of proposals, including a strategy that had been mooted in one of the off-site business proposals. The proposal was to undertake a fair amount of our processing and technology in a different, more cost-effective environment (which in this case, after a detailed search, was determined to be Scotland). In the end, all the time committed by this dedicated group of people had been more than cost-effective: while the initial operation in Scotland required upfront investment, after a relatively short period of time they had covered all the cost of that investment. Now their recommendations are continuing to return a serious amount of money to the firm. That's a significant benefit.

But there are other things that we've learnt as well. First, other parts of the firm decided that they could benefit from the same operating model, so the model of alternative sourcing has popped up in Australia and in the United States. Second, we instigated a way of thinking about our business and an enthusiasm in a group of people who didn't think they had the leeway to go ahead and make a difference. Their excitement about striving to change the business was almost as valuable as the actual net savings the firm has achieved over the same period of time.

It was a great revelation to all of us that, despite being told that a solution couldn't be found, we stuck with it, we got the right people in the room, we encouraged them to focus on the right things, we gave them the latitude to make some interesting choices, and we allowed them to go ahead and run with the strategy. The benefits have been positive both for the company and the individuals involved, as demonstrated by the way in which they have developed as a very strong group of managers.

When you take time to encourage and inspire a group of people to think outside the box, to be creative, and you give them the room to grow, they do just that. People can achieve extraordinary things, but it does take some courage on their part, and on the part of senior management. It also takes a fair amount of commitment in terms of time to encourage them and to allow them the freedom to push the boundaries, but in doing so they grow, because they know that they did it themselves.

What I learned, and I think we all learned as a result, is: 'Never say die.' And if I come back to my Aunt Rebecca, it really is about 'putting your best foot forward and keeping it there'. Whether you're fishing or whether you're growing your business, the areas of focus, commitment, determination and follow-through – which this extraordinary group of individuals showed clearly over a period of time – are essential. They are essential in your personal life, and they are essential in your business life. I think our team now does put its best foot forward and keeps it there.

Executive Timeline Amelia Fawcett

1974–1978	Degree in history, Wellesley College, USA.
1978–1980	**Sullivan & Cromwell** *Paralegal* Major New York law firm
1980–1983	University of Virginia School of Law (JD)
1983–1986	**Sullivan & Cromwell** *Lawyer* Worked in New York and Paris.
1987	**Morgan Stanley** Joined the London office of this large, international financial services firm. She has since been with the firm, and in London, for more than 18 years.
1990	*Vice President*
1992	*Executive Director*
1996	*Managing Director and Chief Administrative Officer* for the European operations
2002–present	**Morgan Stanley International** *Vice Chairman*

Engaging people
on the front line
and supporting the
management in charge
of them is the most
important thing a leader
can do.

5 **The Front Line is the Bottom Line**
Julia Cleverdon

Chief Executive Officer, *Business in the Community*

My Career

I went to a girls' grammar school in Camden, north London, where the motto was 'Onwards and upwards'. We wore the motto on our cap badges, and the bus conductors used to shout: 'Onwards and upwards, Camden girls – we don't want you on the bottom deck!' So I think the motto had quite a strong influence on me. I went to Cambridge University, where I read history and got very involved in student politics. When I graduated I applied for lots of jobs, and couldn't decide whether to become an Assistant Governor in a prison, or an Assistant Secretary in a hospital in Liverpool. My tutor sent me to see someone she felt could help me decide, and he said to me: 'My dear girl, I don't know what you think you're doing dealing with the blind, the sick, the lame and the criminal at the age of twenty-two; you're not nearly old enough. The real problem we are facing is how to persuade free people to create goods and services in industry and commerce. You ought to be in industry.'

As a result of talking to him and of various other influences, I found my way to British Leyland's body and assembly plant in Swindon as their most junior Industrial Relations Officer. I later moved to join the Industrial Society, as it was providing industrial relations communication advice; they sent me to South Africa, where I worked for Anglo-American Mining. It was at a time when the company was beginning to develop black trade unions by encouraging the evolution of black consultative committees throughout its plants. I then returned to the Industrial Society and was put in place as an early leader in charge of all the work they were developing in the public service. I ran a campaign that encouraged industry to explain what it did and how it did it, and then spent eight or ten years in charge of providing communication advisory work, often by working within the companies concerned.

In 1988 I moved to Business in the Community to see how companies could be encouraged to become more involved in tackling some of the issues attendant at times of enormously high youth unemployment, the problems of ethnic minority recruitment and the real difficulties in our inner cities. I've been the Chief Executive since 1992, and I am having a fascinating time seeing how companies have changed the ways in which they do business, how they make a more positive impact on society, in their workplace, in their marketplace and in their community environment.

Julia Cleverdon

Chief Executive Officer, *Business in the Community*

The Front Line is the Bottom Line

Throughout my career I have been fascinated by whether companies recognize that the front line is the bottom line. It should be what matters most in all organizations. The front line of an organization needs to understand the issues, the challenges, and the need for flexibility, accuracy and efficiency in order to produce the goods it says it is going to produce at the time it says it is going to produce them.

I started my working life at British Leyland's body and assembly plant, where I realized very early on that the front line was the bottom line. I started as a very junior Industrial Relations Officer in a motor-car plant that employed 27,000 people on one site and had thirty-two different trade unions. I had the most junior job in the place; there was nobody more junior than me apart from the industrial relations department's cat! In the mornings I carried notebooks into meetings for the shop stewards to record details of negotiations, and in the afternoons I stamped the time-keeping cards. After six months or so of stamping the time-keeping cards, I realized that people who reported to 'Smith' were sick more often than those who reported to 'Brown'; and if you moved Smith to lead Brown's team, the lot that were well got sick, and the lot that were sick got well.

The front-line leadership – that is the team leader responsible for managing the team, who is accountable for achieving results on the front line – is the single most important character in the whole operation, influencing whether or not

The most important person is the one at the highest level who knows the front line, because that's where success or failure hinges.

the team will deliver results. So whenever consultants say to me: 'Oh, the person at the top is very important – they set the whole tone,' I always think that, in fact, the most important person is the one at the highest level who knows the front line because that's where success or failure hinges, and that is where you can actually make things happen.

One of the other places where I realized that the front line was the bottom line was at a railway station in the early hours of the morning. I was working for the Industrial Society in those days, and, having missed my return train to London, I was standing on Peterborough station at about one o'clock in the morning waiting for the milk train to go through at three a.m. The only thing to watch was the sorting of the mail. It was a nightly pantomime that used to run at every single train station across Britain. You would have a British Rail official standing on the train, and you'd have a Royal Mail official standing on the platform. British Rail threw the bags and Royal Mail took the decision as to their destination. I stood there watching the process, as I've always been fascinated by what happens in front-line decision-taking – not decisions taken at Board level, but how the people at the front line take decisions.

At this station the officials were sorting mail to go either west to Wales or north to Scotland. As British Rail shouted out where the bag was to go, Royal Mail took the decision as to which truck it should be put into. The conversation went: 'Aberdare?' 'Aberdare.' 'Abersoch?' 'Abersoch.' 'Aberaeron?' 'Aberaeron.' Aberystwyth?' 'Aberystwyth.' 'Aberdeen?' 'Aberdeen.' And every single bag went straight into the Welsh truck. I leant forward and said: 'I'm frightfully sorry to get in the way, but I think that Aberdeen is in Scotland, and therefore I suspect that that bag should have gone in the Scottish truck, not the Welsh truck.' The two representatives of each of these mighty organizations swung on their heels and looked at me and said: 'Are you trying to teach us how to do our jobs?' I said: 'No, no way; I just feel terribly sorry for all the people who put a first-class stamp on the letter in the hope that, you know, he would get the birthday card in the morning, or she would get the letter that said: "I'm sorry for what I said on the phone, darling," or the income tax return would arrive one day earlier to save the overdraft. Because that's what it's all about,' I said, 'it's about accuracy and efficiency and producing the goods you said you were going to produce, at the time you said you were going to produce them.' They looked at me with pity – and wouldn't move the bag. That picture remains with me forever.

The question is: how do you get the front-line people to care about what they do and how they do it? Finding the answer has been a driving passion for me. By and large the front line knows exactly what ought to be done; it's just that nobody's

By and large the front line knows exactly what ought to be done; it's just that nobody's bothered to ask them much.

bothered to ask them much. Communication is of vital importance; consultation is of vital importance.

Paper is patient. Paper will still be there when the people have gone. Seize the moment to talk to your people; catch a sales team coming back from a successful pitch or, even more important, catch them coming back from an unsuccessful pitch. You've got to get alongside people and understand where they are on the core issues and the deals in that moment, not sit in an office studying the computer returns, which by and large measure yesterday's failure, not tomorrow's opportunities.

Be *with* people, work alongside them; don't just have their actions mapped out in the diary, go out to reception or go and walk the job in the areas of the office that are furthest away from where you normally go to get a cup of coffee and try to understand what it feels like to work there. Ask: 'Are we clear about our customers' needs?' 'Do we know what we did with them?' 'Have we won?' For me, the front line is the bottom line, and the leadership at the front line safeguards the bottom line. The support of that front-line leadership is the single most important responsibility of any management.

1972	**British Leyland** *Industrial Relations Officer* British Leyland was a major motor manufacturing company.
1973	**The Industrial Society** *Industrial Relations Division*
1974	Seconded to work with Anglo-American Mining in South Africa.
1978	Set up Pepperell Development Case for Women.
1981–1988	*Director: Education and Inner City Division* The Industrial Society became the Work Foundation in 2002. It is a not-for-dividend public interest company, which exists to help improve the quality of working life.
1988	**Business in the Community**
1992–present	*Chief Executive Officer* BITC is a unique movement of over 700 of the UK's top companies committed to improving their positive impact on society.

Showing the human face of management by thanking employees for the good work they are doing can generate valuable goodwill and improve performance.

6a **The Humble Boss**
Lord MacLaurin

Chairman, *Vodafone Group*; former Chairman, *Tesco*

My Career

" My schooldays were among the most important times of my
life. I went to school in Malvern in Worcestershire and was
a boarder between the ages of thirteen and eighteen. I was
a proficient sportsman, so was fortunate enough to captain
the cricket side, the soccer side and the rugger side for my last
two years there. By that means I started to learn about people
and their strengths and weaknesses. Malvern gave me a very,
very good education, which sent me off into the wide world.
From there I could have gone to university, but instead I had
to do National Service. I joined the Air Force, where I again
played soccer and cricket and didn't really serve our country
very well. I was one of the last lot to go into National Service
and I found it was good fun. I started to meet all sorts of
different people and suddenly felt I was getting into the real
world. The experience taught me a lot about human nature
and mixing with and understanding people.

I joined Tesco in 1959 as their first trainee, and worked my way
through the operation to become Managing Director and then
Chairman. I left Tesco in 1997 to join Vodafone, and became
Chairman in 1999. I'm now also Chair of the Governors
of my old school. In this day and age it is very unusual for
somebody to spend the majority of their working life, nearly
forty years in my case, in one company, starting first as a
trainee and finishing up as Chairman. These days, people
chop and change their jobs quite regularly, but I had the great
privilege of working with a company and turning it round, and
creating probably one of the strongest retail brands in this

country today. Tesco is a major force in world retailing. Then to have the opportunity to work with Chris Gent to create a world business at Vodafone has meant that I have had a very interesting career. I'm very lucky in lots of ways, and the experience has been thoroughly enjoyable.

Lord MacLaurin

Chairman, *Vodafone Group*; former Chairman, *Tesco*

I learnt very early on in my career that the most humble person in the organization is always the most important.

A valuable business lesson that I learnt very early on in my career is that the most humble person in the organization is always the most important. Never ever forget that. If you're the Chairman and you go into a store and talk to the back-doorman, or chat to the cleaner, they can go home and say: 'Do you know, the Chairman was in today and he was asking me how the family were and he was chatting to me.' They feel good about it.

People management is about getting close to people and avoiding having an arrogant attitude that suggests when you walk into the store that you think you're God's gift to retailing. Nobody is ever that, whatever business you're in. In my experience at Tesco, or during my more recent experience at Vodafone, I've always said to all my managers: 'You need to chat to people and ask them how they are.'

Retailing is a very tough business, and at the end of the day people are very tired. Tesco is open twenty-four hours a day now, but we used to close at eight or ten p.m. On a Friday night I would be in one of the stores at closing time and I would stand at the back door to say thank you to the manager and the staff. By the time I left the company we had about 800 stores, so I couldn't get round them all in a year, but I used to write to each manager following my visits to say: 'Thank you very much, great to see the store. You're really doing a very good job for us and just thank everybody for the job they're doing.' It's human touches, the saying 'thank you' and acknowledging people, that breathe the spirit into and through the company.

Senior managers need to get out of the boardroom and on to the shop floor if the vision they have for the business is to become a reality.

To communicate your vision of your business and to win staff loyalty you've actually got to get out of the boardroom and be seen at the coalface.

In order to communicate your vision of your business and to win staff loyalty you've actually got to get out of the boardroom and be seen out there at the coalface. In the case of Tesco, the senior management team had to go round the stores. Managers need to talk to their staff on a very regular basis. During a typical working week I would be out and around the stores on Tuesday and Friday, and on Saturday morning. One of the things I enjoyed the most was sitting in the staffroom having a cup of tea with people, asking them questions and talking to them about the business.

There was no hierarchy in Tesco. Everyone knew who the Chairman was, and who the Managing Director was, but they were comfortable sitting down and chatting to us about the business. There was no 'Yes, sir; no, sir; three bags full, sir.' When the senior management team had completed their tour of the stores, talking to staff and customers, we would be ready, when we returned to the office on a Monday, to trawl through our experiences of the weekend, to discuss how the stores were and what we had learnt from the conversations. Each person brought his or her own views back to the table.

By getting out into the business, you get to *know* the business. There are those who ask: 'How did you do it? How did you manage to transform the business?' Well, we were active within it. All the top people spent time in the stores and enthusing the staff. If your business is progressing well, you can see the results in the numbers coming through; it means you're communicating well, that people understand what you're trying to do and that they all feel a part of this large team.

If your business is progressing well, you can see the results in the numbers coming through; it means you're communicating well, that people understand what you're trying to do and that they all feel a part of the team.

I think there are about 200,000 people now working for Tesco around the world. When I left the business the figure was about 160,000. All 160,000 knew clearly what the vision was for the business, and how the company was going forward. They knew the level of success the business was experiencing, and they knew that if they worked hard and the company continued to be successful, there was something in it for them at the end of the day.

All 160,000 people knew clearly what the vision was for the business, and how the company was going forward.

To achieve this we had to communicate well with people on a personal level when we went round the stores, and meet them on a very regular basis to let them know what our vision was for the business so they could buy into it too. "

Executive Timeline Lord MacLaurin

1959	**Tesco**
	Management Trainee
	Joined the supermarket chain as its first management trainee.
1970	Appointed to the Board of Directors.
1973–1985	*Managing Director*
1985–1997	*Chairman*
1989	Awarded a knighthood
1996	Awarded a life peerage
1997	**Vodafone Group**
	Appointed to the Board of Directors.
2000–present	*Chairman*
	Chairman of the Nominations and Governance Committee
	Member of the Remuneration Committee

Being a visible leader is important – especially in a multinational organization. A closed-door policy never works because the leader will be cut off from the organization. It is vital to make time for daily, face-to-face communication with your staff. A leader who is never seen will not be recognized.

7

Visible Leadership
Sir Richard Evans

Chairman, *United Utilities*; former Chairman, *British Aerospace*

My Career

I have spent most of my working life in the aerospace business, but I came into it from a humble beginning. When I was starting out I never thought that I had received any guidance in the shaping and development of my career. Having become a bit smarter later on, I came to realize that there is a degree of organization within companies that tends to single people out and monitor their performance to see whether they have what it takes to move into more senior positions. Most of the moves I've made, particularly in the early stages of senior management, came as big surprises to me; they were not appointments that I'd ever imagined I would take at the time that I took them.

The really big move came when I was made Chief Executive of British Aerospace. I think it's fair to say that had I known at the time what I was walking into, I might have thought somewhat longer and harder about whether I should take the job. It was a seriously difficult assignment, with an immense number of problems that I didn't understand when I took on the role. Indeed, I don't think the company really understood quite what the issues were.

I spent longer in the Chief Executive's slot inside British Aerospace and then BAE Systems than I'd ever expected to. At that time the natural progression would have been for the Chief Executive to move on, and to take up a Chairmanship. I had never intended to become Chairman of British Aerospace; I took on the role on account of a set of domestic situations that arose for the then Chairman, Bob Bowman. Bob was an American, and he had to leave the UK to go back to the States. We didn't have time to undertake the usual search and selection process, so I came into the Chairmanship not as a part of conscious succession planning, but as an emergency interim appointment. A similar situation applied at United Utilities. I had been a Non-executive Director at United Utilities for a relatively short period of time when, tragically, the then Chairman of the company died very suddenly. My home was, and still is, in the northwest of England, where United Utilities is based. After first testing the market, the Board asked me if I would step up from my Non-executive position to become Chairman of the company.

I finished up at the top of two FTSE 100 companies via a set of circumstances that were complete chance. I had originally anticipated that, having finished my term as Chief Executive in British Aerospace, I would be able to regain control of my life and spend more time with my wife and family. That's still what I'm trying to achieve, but it's not proving to be as easy as I had expected.

Sir Richard Evans

Chairman, *United Utilities*; former Chairman, *British Aerospace*

Visible Leadership

It's important to me that people see the leader around the organization. If you're controlling a vast multinational, you should be seen around it as often as possible.

I'm a great believer in visibility in leadership. It's important to me that people see the leader around the organization. If you're controlling a vast multinational, you should be seen around it as often as possible. Simple physical limitations will restrict the amount of time that can be spent in different parts of the building, but when I walk in to my office in the morning, I like people to see me arrive, I like to say hello to people and ask them what they have they been doing at the weekend so that they know I'm there. I like them to see that I'm working reasonably hard on their and the shareholders' behalf, and providing the sort of leadership that they will want to follow.

I dislike any form of leadership that closes itself off behind an office door. I've always operated a very clear policy of never shutting my office door, unless there's a fairly big meeting taking place. If it's a small meeting, rarely do I close the office door. That conveys a message. I have an aversion to working in buildings where everybody is sitting in individual offices: those are places where people hide. They go in there to keep

Invariably, as you progressed through the organization, you ended up with an office on the 'Golden Mile'. Managers had made it to the top of the organization, but could barely see from one end of the corridor to the other.

out of the way and out of sight: such action speaks volumes about the quality of a person in leadership terms.

In my early days in senior management we were housed in a grandiose, purpose-built building in outer London. There were two wonderful long corridors in this building: one was appropriately entitled the 'Silver Mile', and the other the 'Golden Mile'. Invariably, as you progressed through the organization, you ended up with an office on the 'Golden Mile'. Managers had made it to the top of the organization, but could barely see from one end of the corridor to the other. No one ever saw another person walking along it. The first time I was located there to work I suggested that we should pipe in some organ music because it was like walking into a funeral parlour. Everybody had a wonderful office, but there were no open doors. You never saw a warm body while you were in the building, and it was the most soulless place imaginable. The working people never saw the management or the leadership of the business. Now that is utterly horrendous. My instinct was just to rip the walls down – until it was explained to me that the building would collapse if we did so. Others said it could cost too much to relocate to another building to work in. What complete rubbish! In fact, money would be saved because, provided management visibility improved, performance would improve.

If you want to make leadership work, first of all the leader has to be visible. A leader who is never seen will not be recognized as a leader.

If you want to make leadership work, first of all the leader has to be visible. A leader who is never seen will not be recognized as a leader. To be a visible leader takes work, and you've got to make time for it. You've got an office to run, you've got to keep the in-tray moving, you've got to take the telephone calls – but you've also got to make time to get around and go around. If it's a large organization, the leader needs to be prepared to do a lot of travelling.

Anybody who wants to sit inside a closed office along a passageway is not for me. If you want people to follow

To be a visible leader takes work, and you've got to make time for it.

you, they've got to be able to see you and they've got to be able to talk to you. If that is not your style, then get out of management and go and do something else. **"**

1960	**Ministry of Transport and Civil Aviation**
1967	**Ferranti**
	Government Contracts Officer
	Ferranti was a global organization known for technological innovation. It closed in 1994 after one hundred years of trading.
1969	**British Aircraft Corporation**
	Joined the Military Aircraft Division.
1978	*Commercial Director* – Warton Division, British Aerospace (BAe)
1981	*Assistant Managing Director* – Warton Division
1983–1986	*Deputy Managing Director*
	Appointed following BAe Aircraft Group managerial changes.
1986	*Deputy Managing Director (and Managing Director Designate)* – British Aerospace Military Aircraft Division
1987	*Marketing Director* – British Aerospace
	Appointed to the Board.
1988	*Chairman* – British Aerospace Defence companies
1990	*Chief Executive* – British Aerospace
1996	Knighted in the 1996 Queen's Birthday Honours.
1997	**United Utilities**
	Joined the Board as a Non-executive Director. United Utilities manages water and wastewater networks in Wales and wastewater treatment facilities in Scotland.
1998–2004	*Chairman* – British Aerospace
	Continued to chair the company when it became BAE Systems following the merger with Marconi Electronic Systems. Retired from this position in July 2004, but continues to support the company in an advisory capacity.
2001–present	**United Utilities**
	Chairman

> To gain authority and stature within an organization, an executive must appear to be all-seeing and all-knowing. Being omnipotent and always seeming relaxed breeds lasting confidence within employees.

8a   The Omnipotent Boss
Lord Kalms

President, *Dixons Group*

My Career

" I started my career in 1948 working with my father. We had a couple of shops that quickly reduced to one, and then I started my career with Dixons. It's a career that has been totally focused and based on a very simple philosophy of expanding the business slowly. We floated Dixons in 1962, and from that moment onwards the company has been in continuous growth. Today we have 1400 stores and we trade in thirteen different countries.

Following flotation, I focused on expanding Dixons' inventory and made many small acquisitions. By the middle of the 1980s we had about 300 stores. I then made my biggest acquisition, hard fought, which was to buy Currys, the electrical retail chain.

Taking over Currys was a breakthrough. It put us into the white goods business, and since then it's been a question of consolidating and growing and growing. Today we employ some 35,000 people, which makes it quite a large organization. We've been a FTSE company for a number of years.

During our period of growth, I have concentrated on maintaining high standards, while being very conscious of other interests. We've broadened the base of our social responsibilities, and have been very involved in education. In my own community I have personally funded the building of schools. I try to keep the company focused on social responsibilities as well as wealth creation, and I've achieved that with a modicum of success.

Lord Kalms

Dixons' City Technology College in Bradford is the apple of my eye, and a wonderful example of how business can relate to, and make a major contribution to, a community. I am passionate about the big role that business should play in a community.

I was given a knighthood in 1996 for services to my industry. I've also been very involved within the political arena. I am passionate about Europe and not giving in to the bureaucracy and the autonomy of Brussels. I fought very strongly to keep the pound against the euro. I founded Business for Sterling in the 1990s, which turned out to be one of the most powerful lobby groups ever and influenced the CBI, which favoured the euro, in its decision to become neutral. The lobby group managed to persuade business that the euro was not good for the UK, and my political involvement continued. I ended up as Treasurer of the Conservative Party – a pretty tough job – and as a result of that I was given a peerage in June 2004. I've been fairly successful and am glad to have been highly regarded. I also have quite a few honorary degrees.

Lord Kalms

President, *Dixons Group*

My concern was how to have real authority when running a business.

One of my strategies when, at sixteen or seventeen years old, I started to build a business was always to employ people much older than myself. My concern was how to have real authority when running a business. I came to the conclusion very early on that I had to appear to be omnipotent. I had to appear to be wise, clever, successful, authoritative, far-seeing, wealthy – all the things that give employees confidence. Very early on I learnt the technique of always appearing to be relaxed, sensible, unconcerned about events and able to control issues. I focused on giving that impression to my staff all the time, and there were instances of it happening every day: when people came in full of their woes I would always have an answer.

I remember a dramatic instance during those early days, when the government imposed horrendous financial restrictions on credit. We used to operate a large hire-purchase business, and the government decided overnight that companies like ours needed to take a one-third deposit from customers. We were asking for only a 10 per cent deposit at the time, so I was anticipating a major negative impact on my business. Everybody in the shop was very glum, so I asked someone to get hold of the actual regulation.

I learnt the technique of always appearing to be relaxed, sensible, unconcerned about events and able to control issues.

I sat at my desk and studied it closely. Within an hour I called everybody together and said: 'I have found a loophole in this regulation, and in fact we can still offer credit over nine months in equal instalments.' This might sound like a detail, but it was a major breakthrough. It changed horrendous thoughts that our business would be decimated into an awareness that not only could we continue developing, but I had also found a better way of setting up the agreements. That was how I earned people's respect. They thought: 'He found the loophole; this is a good boss to be with.'

Bosses need to have eyes in the back of their head; creating an informal network that delivers both good and bad news is the way to stay well informed.

The Internal Grapevine

In order to become a good boss, a good grapevine system is needed; and to achieve that a boss needs a lot of mates in the business.

Knowledge is the most important thing that the boss can have. The boss has to know everything that goes on in the business. He or she has to have eyes in the back of his head, and be very sensitive, watching and being aware of everything that's happening. If he's in the shop, he has to see every customer, watch whether they leave without buying, and, if they do, make an enquiry afterwards.

In order to become a good boss, a good grapevine system is needed; and to achieve that a boss needs a lot of mates in the business. A boss needs to know people throughout the business whom he trusts, who like him, who will talk to him, will gossip with him on the phone and who feel relaxed with him. In this way a flow of information will develop. A network is particularly important as the business grows and moves outside the leader's immediate control.

In organizing the large company that Dixons became, one of my skills was to operate via key committees; these enabled me to control the business. I'm not a bureaucrat, but I do find that running certain committees and keeping proper minutes provides a very good discipline for running a large company. When I was the Chief Executive, I used to have the Chief

Executive Committee; later on this became the Chairman's Committee, and was task oriented. The senior management would come in, discuss matters and be allocated jobs. Conversations and action points would be minuted, and the results of those actions had to be reported back to the next meeting. I had half a dozen key committees running the business, but I would have to say that they are important only if you have a very big, strong, informal system that works too.

The best way to run a business is to leave your door wide open so that anybody feels able to come in at any time. It was years and years before I showed any resistance to people just barging into my office. Eventually I just had to introduce some discipline, but it was still possible to see me quickly, on the same day, if the matter was important. My door was always open because staying well-informed is about talking to people.

I make it the rule that bad news always has to be given to me instantly. I don't care about good news. Don't phone me up and tell me you made a good sale: phone me up when something's gone wrong so that I know I've got a crisis on my hands. People learnt that they could speak to me, officially or unofficially, so I was always made aware instantly of what was going on in the business. I think that carried on even when we had 30,000 or so people. I could always rely on enough people in the company to chat with me to ensure I was aware of problems. I worry only about problems. I don't mind waiting to receive good news as it will still be there the following morning.

In a large business the boss has to walk the floor, he has to be available – and then it's amazing what he'll learn. Part of my grapevine system is to walk around and lean over the desk of somebody and ask: 'What's that you are doing?' Then I would tell them a better way of doing it. That's a great secret. There are dangers to that approach of course, because the boss is a very powerful personality and the young people don't always appreciate his forcefulness, his friendliness and his approachability. There is always the danger that they might take what you have said too literally.

Just to emphasize this particular point – I remember looking at some products in one of our catalogues and remarking in my usual style to a new young buyer who'd put together a lovely range of watches: 'What a load of **** they are,' thinking that he would defend them. Most people knew me and would defend their decisions because they knew that I was just probing them. My new buyer looked at the watches, listened to The Boss and panicked. The next I knew about it was that all the watches had been taken out of the catalogue. That taught me a lesson. If leaders adopt a challenging style of management, they have got to be careful that the person they're talking to can take the stick.

At the end of the day, leaders need to recognize that the only thing that matters in a business is the people who are in it, and it's how you actually work with people that matters.

Executive Timeline Lord Kalms

1937	**Dixons** founded as Dixon Studios Ltd.
1948	Began career working for father.
	Grew Dixons from the one-store family business and turned it into Europe's leading electrical retailer.
1962	Dixons flotation.
Until 1971	*Chief Executive*
1971–2002	**Dixons Group**
	Chairman
1984	Acquisition of Currys
	Currys was the UK's largest electrical retailer.
1996	Awarded a knighthood in recognition of services to the electrical retailing industry.
2002	*Life President*
	Stepped down from the Board to become Life President.
2004	Awarded a life peerage.

All leaders, in all situations, have to make tough calls. Don't shy away from making those decisions; be ready to stand up and be counted. You don't need to win a popularity contest, so don't confuse being popular with the need to make the right choices.

9a **Leadership is not a Popularity Contest**
Sanjiv Ahuja

Chief Executive Officer, *Orange Group*

My Career

 I completed an undergraduate degree in electrical engineering and then went to the United States, where I did a Masters at Columbia University in New York. I went to work for IBM in 1979. I grew through the ranks and became a mid-level executive leading one of IBM's software businesses. I left IBM in 1994 to go to Bell Communications Research and was there until 2000. I left as the President of the company. I then moved into the venture capital business for a couple of years before I came to Orange. I've been the Chief Executive Officer of Orange since early 2004.

Sanjiv Ahuja

Chief Executive Officer, *Orange Group*

As a leader of a business, be very clear in your mind that you are not running a democracy; leaders must be prepared to exercise the authority that comes with a leadership role.

There is a big myth in business: that you need your team to buy into your strategy. There is another big myth: that leaders need to win a popularity contest inside their company. As a leader of a business, be very clear in your mind that you are not running a democracy; leaders must be prepared to exercize the authority that comes with a leadership role.

When you make decisions, when you make choices, they will not always be the most popular choices. If your objective is to ensure that your team buys into your strategy or likes what you do, then you are not needed as a leader. You could operate a continuous poll of ideas to determine what decision and what direction the company ought to move in; you could do that from morning to night. Everybody would work on it and the business would be rudderless.

As a leader you are supposed to make some decisions that aren't necessarily going to be very popular and that is okay; but stand up and be counted for those decisions. Sometimes decisions are needed that will put your job on the line; but that's okay too – stand up and be counted for those decisions.

When you look at the history of mankind, all successful leaders at different stages of their life have had to make those types of decisions. If these become 'bet your job' decisions, that's okay; people make 'bet your life' decisions every day. Most of the decisions we make are not that critical; but we must still make them and not be deluded by the absolute myth that it is necessary to be a popular leader. You need to be an *effective* leader, you need to be a *decisive* leader, but once you are leading with effectiveness, decisiveness, clarity and a passion for the success of your business, your team will follow you.

Sometimes decisions are needed that will put your job on the line; but that's okay – stand up and be counted for those decisions.

Around ten years ago I was brought into a business where employee morale was low, product quality was poor and profits were in a terrible shape. The revenue had been in decline for a number of years. Most of the customers doubted that the business could be turned around; a few of the employees thought that too. When I stepped in I had to make a significant number of changes. I changed most of the leadership team, I changed a good portion of the management team that worked for those leaders; essentially I restructured the business.

Once you are leading with effectiveness, decisiveness, clarity and a passion for the success of your business, your team will follow you.

In the early days I wasn't the most popular leader, but by the time we had completed the transformation the company was delivering world-class performance in terms of quality, delivery, productivity, profitability and growth. The company met all performance criteria in a world-class manner and I would like to say that by the time I left I was probably the most popular leader that company had ever had. Had I been looking for employee accolades, I probably would not have taken any of the tough decisions that I had to take.

All leaders, in all situations, have to make the tough calls. Don't shy away from making those calls; be ready to stand up and be counted. Don't confuse popularity with the need to make the right choices. Right choices and popularity do not have to go hand in hand.

A leader who is true
to his or her personal
values creates a personal
'brand' of leadership.
Clear communication
of leadership values
provides people with
decision-making criteria
that are understood and
encourage world-class
performance.

9b   **Establish your Personal Brand**

A brand represents values: it means all the values associated with the product, service or person are obvious.

Just as all successful products and services are branded, so too it is essential that you as a leader have a brand. What does 'brand' mean? A brand represents values: it means all the values associated with the product, service or person are obvious. A brand should be consistent time after time, day in and day out, year after year, so that people are able to recognize what it is that this individual, this leader, in whatever endeavour they are engaged, stands for.

Leaders can be demanding; leaders can expect a lot from their team. Leaders can be hard working, they can be decisive or they can demonstrate innovation. Leaders can also sometimes be negative. Every individual, every leader in the history of mankind has stood for certain things. One of the first things that I did when I became CEO of Orange was to talk to my teams. I spoke to all the people who reported to me in all the different countries. I told each of the teams what I stood for. I told them what they could count on me for, day in and day out; I told them how I would react to situations when they talked to me. I laid it out, I was clear; I put it on the table.

Simultaneously, I laid out my expectations of them. I talked about world-class performance; I told them that I am very demanding, that I am passionate, that I stand for Orange values, that I would stand up for the team and that I deliver to my own expectations. Then I said I expect world-class performance from them in return: day in and day out. Having told them what I stand for, and what their expectations should be, I could then equally and clearly state my demands and set my expectations of the team, and expect that it would get done because I provided clarity.

I told each of the teams what I stood for. I told them how I would react to situations when they talked to me.

Sometimes in business there are pressures to get a product to market before it is ready. Market pull is attempting to bring the product out sooner than it's ready, and there might even be an internal move to *push* the product out before the right time. As a leader, if you stand for quality, you have to step up and say: 'We will not ship the product before it's ready.' We take that stance within Orange.

Sometimes our focus on quality may mean that our product or service launches are delayed. We are not always first to the market. We were not first to the marketplace with 3G in either the UK or in France; we got it out when it was ready. We said we wouldn't ship it and we wouldn't deliver it to our customers until it was ready and so we didn't. Those are tough decisions to make, especially when hundreds of

Do not ever compromise your personal values ... because it's much harder to re-establish them than it is to establish them the first time around.

millions to billions of euros are invested in an activity and your decision is: 'I am not going to do it. I will take the impact on the business. I am not going to do it until it delivers the right customer experience.'

Such a decision is a reflection of your business values and of your personal values. If your team sees you being true to your values and knows you will take that approach on big decisions, then you provide clear decision-making criteria for your team to live by, and you lead along a clearly established path. Your people will never come back and question your values. When they are making their decisions on a daily basis, they can use the same value filter for their own decision-making: that leads to more empowered teams, which leads to quicker decisions, and that leads to clarity and efficiency.

Once you have established a 'brand' value for yourself and stated what your personal brand stands for, live up to it, day in and day out. Do not ever compromise your personal values or your brand values, because it's much harder to re-establish them than it is to establish them the first time around.

Executive Timeline Sanjiv Ahuja

Early Years	Degree in electrical engineering, Delhi University, India.
	Masters Degree Columbia University, New York.
1979–1994	**IBM**
	Various executive roles, including leading IBM's entry into the telecommunications software industry.
	IBM is a major multinational company, specializing in computer hardware and software, and in providing IT consultancy.
1994–2000	**Bell Communications Research**
	President
	Bell is the world's largest provider of operations support systems, network software and consulting and engineering services to the telecommunications industry.
2000–2002	Venture capital businesses
2003–2004	**Orange Group**
	Chief Operating Officer
2004–present	*Chief Executive Officer*

Emotion is a valuable tool in business. While it is undoubtedly effective in getting your point across, over-using it decreases its impact. Use it sparingly however, and it is a potent addition to your armoury.

10a **Use Emotion Sparingly**
David Michels

Group Chief Executive, *Hilton Group*

My Career

I began my career path as a waiter in Simpson's-in-the-Strand before becoming an assistant to the Assistant Controller in a hotel called the Mostyn in Oxford Street. I spent fifteen years in sales and marketing with the hotel chain Grand Metropolitan, five of which were spent in America. My time with Grand Metropolitan was an instant success that took fifteen years. I finished there as Worldwide Sales and Marketing Director about the time Sir Maxwell Joseph died and the company bought Intercontinental. I then spent ten years with the leisure group Ladbrokes, starting as a Sales Representative for the hotel division, before becoming Managing Director of a gaming machine division for three years, which was fascinating.

Ladbrokes bought Hilton and I became a Senior Vice President of both organizations. I left Ladbrokes in 1981 on 1 April, the same date that I joined the company. There must be a moral in that tale – especially as I returned to Ladbrokes, again on 1 April funnily enough. I left Ladbrokes the first time to become Chief Executive of Stakis plc, an ailing hotel chain in Scotland, with a wonderful brand name and some marvellous people. We moved that company from a market cap of £24 million and sold it to Hilton nine years later for £1.8 billion – so a modicum of success there. I returned to Hilton Ladbrokes, and three years ago became CEO of the Hilton Group.

David Michels

Group Chief Executive, Hilton Group

In business a manager can get excited only so many times a year in order to be effective; and when it happens everything has to quake. Use it once a week and eventually everyone will ignore you.

Emotion is a valuable tool in business, but it has to be used sparingly. I use emotion, whether in anger or fear or anything else that seems appropriate, but in business a manager can get excited only so many times a year in order for the emotion to be effective; and when it happens everything has to quake. Use it once a week and eventually everyone will ignore you. However, there are occasions, particularly when dealing with people who don't know you, when the use of emotion can have a powerful effect.

I was on the Board of Arcadia – the company that was sold two or three years ago to the entrepreneur and retailer Philip Green. The Board was meeting to decide whether to sell the company for a price vastly higher than it had been when most of us had started. Stuart Rose, currently of Marks & Spencer, was the Chief Executive who had been brought in to save the company, and we had a great Chairman called Adam Broadbent. I was simply the Non-executive Director.

At the end of the day the Board has the responsibility for deciding whether to sell the company on, and whether we are doing the right thing for the shareholders. You can't take a straw poll. I wouldn't say the decision was near the cut, but we were fairly certain we needed to sell, when, in the middle of the meeting, Stuart Rose stood up and said: 'I can get us an extra dividend.' The extra dividend was 7p or 8p added on to the share price, but Stuart didn't say it in a calm tone of voice; he was emphatic: 'I CAN GET IT.' It became an emotional challenge. Now I admired Stuart enormously, but he was due to get a huge amount of money anyhow. He said: 'I can go to Philip Green; I can talk him through it and I can get that extra 7p,' multiplied by however many tens of million shares it was. We were all a bit doubtful because it was definitely an emotional outburst rather than a fine money calculation. Off went Stuart. We received a call to come back to the boardroom about six hours later, and Stuart came back with his 7p.

Stuart Rose and Philip Green are both hard businessmen, and although I wasn't there and I didn't witness the conversation I'm absolutely sure it was not a scientific agreement based upon the value, because there was no possibility of a scientific agreement: the Board had more or less reached that conclusion already. It was an emotional response of the 'I have to have this sort of deal, or it won't be done' ilk. Obviously, or willingly – we'll never know – Philip Green was prepared to buy that argument. It is an agreement that could never have been achieved by letter; it could never have been agreed by calculator. That kind of agreement can only be reached using real emotion.

Emotion is a tool you bring out of the toolbox only very, very rarely in business, and its use is instinctive.

I remember trying to inspire one hundred General Managers to stick by a brand name that was not yet famous throughout the UK. The brand was Stakis. I had never used emotion in that way before and I would never do it again. I found myself quoting Martin Luther King and genuinely, without planning, I had tears in my eyes because I really cared. It is not something that you can rehearse unless you're a full-time actor, and that I'm not. I'm trying to be a full-time businessman – and that takes up enough of the time. I really did care; the Managers knew I cared and the impact ricocheted, absolutely ricocheted around the room. On that occasion it was pure emotion. I managed to transfer it from the platform to the audience and back again, which inspired me more. When you can get that degree of electricity purely from emotion, it works.

Emotion is a tool you bring out of the toolbox only very, very rarely in business, and its use is instinctive. It's not something that you can plan to use, or something that should be part of your upfront arsenal. It's just something that's there; something in your brain just ticks and says: 'Use the emotional card.' Be aware, however, that it's the joker in the pack; it's a card you can play only once every fifty-two times.

Often the bigger you get in business, the greater the temptation to ask others' opinion about decisions that need to be made. But beware of putting too much faith in committees and consultants. While they are there to assist the individual in making the right decision, they are not there to make the decision for them.

Beware of Committees

Beware of Committees

It seems that the further a leader progresses in business, and the more one grows in life, the more frequently one wants to ask other people their opinions, get everybody on board, have all the specialists come in, and get all the outside help that can be found.

The tendency to want to consult reminds me of when I was a fairly junior employee at Grand Metropolitan, now called Diageo. Its Chairman at that time, and the founder of the company, was Sir Maxwell Joseph. He did everything on his own. He made all his decisions, and would then phone up his managers to tell them what he'd decided to do. He bought three hotels in Paris one day – the Grande, the Maurice and the Prince De Gaulle – a deal in today's money of at least £250 million. Then he called both me and my boss at the time to say: 'I've just bought three hotels in Paris – will you take care of them?' We were both so scared of him that it was the next day before we had the courage to ask which they were. We almost headed to Paris without knowing the names of the hotels.

Eventually, having bought the freehold of some eighty or ninety hotels, Max must have given in to the enormous pressure coming from his fellow Directors, because he decided to buy the next hotel by committee. The hotel in question was the Royal Manhattan in New York on 44th Street and Lexington, which, thirty years ago, was a terrible place. It was a big hotel, with 1300 bedrooms, and was being sold for a lot of money for the time. The Sales Director and the Finance Director went out there, we asked seventeen consultants to give their opinions, and we did surveys of the customers and the area. Then Max bought the hotel.

It was the only single hotel he ever bought for about $100 million and sold at a loss two years later for $12 million. That doesn't mean that no decision should ever be taken by committee, but it does mean that if a guy has an enormous talent for something – in Max's case, an instinct for property – he doesn't need to ask dozens of other people.

There is a famous story about Sir Maxwell Joseph that I can 99 per cent verify. He was Chairman and Chief Executive, and any other important title in the 1970s. The 1970s were the time of good corporate governance. People knew how to spell it, but they weren't doing it: they knew the words existed and were just beginning to look at the concept. Sir Max had a main Board of about fifteen people. One day he went to the normal Board meeting and informed everybody that he was going to buy – I can't remember the exact figure – about £50 million worth of Savoy shares, which was a lot of money in those days. He just mentioned it in passing. The Board decided for the first time ever to flex a bit of muscle, and found the courage – I don't know where from – to vote 15:1 against Max going out with the company's money to buy

Savoy shares. The vote was duly recorded, yet about an hour and a half after the Board meeting Max went out and bought the shares anyway. True story? Probably...

I'm not sure there is a moral in this tale that is applicable today, but the end of the story is that he turned that money over twice in six months. That doesn't mean there shouldn't be good corporate governance – of course there should be. It doesn't mean that you can go against your Board today; that is an impossibility. However, it does mean that 15:1 is not always right.

Committees and consultants are there to assist the individual in making the right decision – but they are not there to make the decision for the individual. If you have reached a stage in your career where you are being paid to make a decision, make one. **"**

Executive Timeline David Michels

Early career	Graduate – London Hotel School
	Grand Metropolitan
	Worldwide Marketing Director
	Spent fifteen years with the company, mainly in sales and marketing roles.
1981	**Ladbroke Group plc**
	Sales and Marketing Director – Ladbroke Hotels
1983	*Managing Director* – Ladbroke Leisure Division
1985	*Managing Director* – Ladbroke Hotels
1987	**Hilton International**
	Senior Vice President, Sales and Marketing
	Appointed following acquisition of Hilton International by Ladbroke Group.
1989	**Hilton UK**
	Deputy Chairman
	Hilton International
	Executive Vice President
1991	**Stakis plc**
	Chief Executive Officer
	Steered the group to a leading position in the UK hospitality sector.
1999	Stakis acquired by Hilton Group.
March 1999	**Hilton Group** (formerly Ladbroke Group)
	Joined the board.
April 1999	**Hilton International**
	Chief Executive
2000	**Hilton Group**
	Group Chief Executive
	Responsible for Hilton Group/Hilton International Hotels (UK) Ltd/Scandic Hotels AB.

Alongside attention to detail, direct personal involvement and communication with all stakeholders is crucial to leaders running a company. However, giving people the freedom to run their business units autonomously, without interference, is also essential.

11   **Attention to Detail**
Sir Martin Sorrell

Group Chief Executive, *WPP*

My Career

I was born in 1945 and went to Haberdashers' Aske's School in a Jewish community in northwest London. I was granted a place at Cambridge University, but before I went there I had a summer job at the journal *Management Today*, so I'm a frustrated journalist really. At Cambridge I read economics.

I went straight to Harvard Business School after that and had a summer job in the UK at Marks & Spencer. After graduating from Harvard in 1969 I worked for Glendenning Associates – a marketing consultancy in Westport, Connecticut. Then I joined Mark McCormack at IMG – the sports and lifestyle marketing and management company. At the time they managed Arnold Palmer, Gary Player, Jack Nicklaus, Jean-Claude Killy, Jean Shrimpton – the light of my life – and all sorts of other interesting people.

After that I joined James Gulliver of the Argyll Group as a Personal Financial Advisor, which meant that I carried his bags and was his gofer. He made an investment in Saatchi & Saatchi: I met Maurice and Charles Saatchi and became their Chief Financial Officer for nine years. Following my attack of andropause in 1985, I decided to go into business for myself – hence WPP. I'm Chief Executive of WPP, one of the world's largest communications services companies, and it's a job I've been enjoying for twenty years.

Sir Martin Sorrell

Group Chief Executive, *WPP*

I think of the company as being mine, so to have an understanding and knowledge of what's going on inside it is critically important.

A lot of people think they can annoy me or upset me by calling me a micro-manager, but I don't take it as an insult. I think it's a compliment. Attention to detail is critically important. Part of my tendency in this area is due to the fact that I started the company and therefore suffer from 'Founder's Disease'. WPP is very much my baby – or at least I regard it as being my baby – despite the fact that I own a relatively low proportion of the equity. I think of the company as being mine, so to have an understanding and knowledge of what's going on inside it is critically important.

At Saatchi & Saatchi Maurice and Charles Saatchi moved away from the detail of their business. They believed in what they called the 'min-aggro' route, which meant minimum aggravation. This meant that the Directors thought about things, and had people to delegate to, such as Tim Bell on the professional side of the business (the best client man that I've ever come across) and myself on the financial and administrative side. The interesting thing is that if Directors pull too far away from their business and stop exhibiting a true understanding, it is unlikely that they will get back into it.

Like everything in life, management is about balance, but I think I would always err on the side of being involved in the detail and micro-management. If you asked what my central function is and what I should focus on, I would say that my priority is to get the very best people for the business, which we run as fifteen units or operating 'tribes'.

At the same time I need to be involved to some extent with clients and with our people. If I'm not involved, the clients turn around and say: 'You're not interested.' If I'm over-involved with staff, the people running the day-to-day business will say: 'You've hired me to run the business, so let me do it.' Management involves continual stress and strain, and is not easy. Managing and being involved with the clients and people who are the heart of our business is terribly important.

The same principle applies to share-owners. If you isolate yourself from them and say: 'I'm not going to visit Boston or London or wherever they are,' the leadership becomes increasingly isolated. That's not just true of the share-owning community, it's true of everything.

The worst thing you can do is isolate yourself from the Press. When the dreaded journalist calls from the dreaded journal, any journal, and is going to write a nasty piece – a 'minus ten' piece – on WPP (there are often 'minus ten' pieces on WPP), I know that if I speak personally to the journalist, it will make a positive difference: he or she will write a piece

If someone were to ask me what I would like as my epitaph or in my obituary, it would say that I was somebody who not only founded a business, but also managed to run it on a considerable scale.

that is a minus eight or a minus nine. If I don't speak to the journalist, the result could be a minus eleven or a minus twelve. It's no good handing the responsibility to a bevy of communications people inside the company or to an agency. Direct involvement and direct communication is critically important.

Aligned to this belief is another important lesson that I've learned. If someone were to ask me what I would like as my epitaph or in my obituary, it would say that I was somebody who not only founded a business, but also managed to run it on a considerable scale. Starting something is only half of it. It's a bit like buying a company and then not being able to run it. It's very easy to spend money in acquisition, particularly in buoyant economic conditions like the ones we experienced in the 1990s. It's very difficult to make a company operate effectively, and extract the synergies and implement the strategy. Therefore, attention to detail is very important.

Executive Timeline Sir Martin Sorrell

1968	Graduated from Harvard Business School.
1968–1969	**Glendenning Associates**
	US-based marketing consultancy in Westport, Connecticut
1970–1974	**Mark McCormack Organization**
	Managed the business affairs of sports personalities.
1975–1977	**James Gulliver Associates**
	Worked personally for James Gulliver.
1977–1984	**Saatchi & Saatchi**
	Group Finance Director
	Saatchi & Saatchi is an advertising agency group.
1986–present	**WPP Group**
	Group Chief Executive
	WPP is one of the world's largest communications services companies.
	Major brands include advertising agencies JWT Company, Ogilvy & Mather Worldwide and Y&R.

Spotting natural leadership ability is a key to success for those at the top of any organization. Invest time in finding and encouraging people who are motivational leaders, and get them into positions of power quickly.

12   **Devote Your Time to Finding Leaders**
Gerry Robinson

Non-executive Chairman, *Allied Domecq*

My Career

When I left college I had planned to become a priest. Instead, I went along with my mum to Lesney Products and got a job working for Matchbox Toys. I really enjoyed working there. It was a very raw company; I moved around within Matchbox Toys and learnt a great deal. I stayed nine years before moving on to Lex (Transport) Group.

The great thing about Lex was that it was a small company with fantastic ideas about choosing good people, and paying and rewarding them well. At Lex I learnt that if you want something to happen, you have to set out a series of objectives that demonstrate how it can be made to happen. The company was great from that point of view – they employed a lot of very bright, very itchy people.

From Lex I was headhunted to take on the role of Finance Director of Coca-Cola in the UK. Coca-Cola Southern had got itself into quite a mess because it had put another soft drinks company, called Club, together with Coca-Cola. I really enjoyed sorting out the mess. A year later I was offered the great opportunity to become Marketing Director of Coca-Cola – and I threw off my background as 'the finance guy' with great joy. I then became Managing Director of the Coca-Cola operation and I loved it. I had a great, great time.

I then led a buyout of the Compass business from Grand Metropolitan. This was terrific because, in addition to enjoying myself, I made quite a lot of money. It was a good example of how you can change something really quickly if people are behind it – and a lot of us benefited from the reward structure.

Then I became bored. I got bored with the whole catering business. As luck would have it, in 1991 I was approached completely out of the blue to run Granada, the UK-based media and hotel conglomerate. I went along to have a look and I really liked Alex Bernstein (now Lord Bernstein), who was Chairman of Granada, and I had a crack at it. Working in television was a whole new game to me. It was probably the most exciting time in my business career because at Granada there was just so much that I could do, and do very quickly. Along the way I became involved with Sky and ITN; there was a lot happening in both those businesses at the time. Finally, I retired from Granada. Currently I am very much enjoying my role as Non-executive Chairman of Allied Domecq, the international spirits and wine group.

Gerry Robinson

Non-executive Chairman, *Allied Domecq*

Leadership is an attribute. Some people have it, some people don't.

When you are running a large organization, a vital key to making it successful is to ensure that you find people for your management positions who can lead others. You have to devote serious time and energy to finding such people. They are almost certainly already within the organization, but, if not, will be available in the marketplace.

Having a manager who can lead, as opposed to somebody who can't, makes an extraordinary difference to the success of a company, yet many people are frightened to deal with that issue. Leadership is an attribute. Some people have it, some people don't. You can encourage innate leadership skills to develop if the promise is there, but unless you identify the potential leaders within your organization, the organization will not do well. Without effective leaders you will spend more time doing things than you need to; and, worse than that, those with potential will go somewhere else. So the task of finding people within the organization who are capable of leading is crucially important.

I presented a television series recently for BBC TV called *I'll Show Them Who's Boss*. One of the case studies followed the progress of a greengrocery business in the West Country. It was absolutely clear from the outset that none of the three partners was capable of running it, and none of them was leading it. They were very nice – very genuine people – and were very willing to do the right thing. This business had lost money for thirteen or fourteen years, and they were in deep financial trouble. If it hadn't been for the fact they owned some property, they would have closed long before.

The process we went through was to look within the family for leadership potential because I felt – and they certainly felt – there had to be someone from within the family who could turn the business around. We identified somebody who would never have been given the role by other means. He was a third-generation cousin and a van driver at the time. The partners agreed – and it was very brave of them to do so – to let him run it.

Within six months that business was making a profit for the first time in years – and it has gone on to be enormously profitable. All that was required was to find somebody with the right skills, who knew how to lead other people and who had a bit of nous to understand how the business worked. Believe me, the partners weren't lazy: they had been working their socks off for fourteen years. And yet this one man, given six months, transformed the whole thing – and it was because he knew how to lead. He knew how to get other people to do things, he knew how to make decisions quickly, and he knew what was important and what wasn't.

The task of finding people within the organization who are capable of leading is crucially important.

One man, given six months, transformed the whole thing – and it was because he knew how to lead.

If you go into an organization that is in trouble, the first thing to do is to get as many people as possible to present to you what they think the problems are, and what they think they'll do about them. I promise you that within fifteen minutes of listening to each one of them you will be able to tell the 99 per cent who aren't going to do anything, and pick out the one who is. It's amazingly clear and straightforward – that person simply talks sense.

Leadership is a strange skill, and needs to be separated from whether or not the person makes good judgements. There are leaders who have been brilliant at getting people to follow them but who have made terrible judgements, from Hitler downwards. The capacity to lead is the capacity to persuade other people to want to do what you want them to do. In my view, it is an inherent quality, and if coupled with some business nous, it's a fantastic combination. The worst thing you can have is somebody with tremendous leadership skills but very little business acumen because they can take you and everyone else into some terrible situations.

The leadership spark, and it *is* a spark, is very specific to particular individuals. Some people have it and some don't. If you haven't got it, you are likely to struggle if you are put into a leadership role.

Generally, you don't have to encourage leaders – they emerge, particularly if you are looking out for them. Most people who have the capacity to lead want to lead. Not all of them do, though. Occasionally you do find somebody who is very capable, but, for whatever reason, simply doesn't want to take on the role, and then you have to encourage him or her. Leaders need to be encouraged in the usual way. You notice when they do things properly, and you reward them for success. It's extraordinary how the powerful impact of a simple 'well done' is underestimated – no matter how senior you are, or think you are, when someone says to you: 'That was great,' you feel terrific. So motivating future leaders is often about recognizing what they've done.

Looking for a leader is top of my list of management priorities.

Nearly everything appears to resolve itself if you have the right person running the show. If you have the wrong person running it, nothing you do is really going to solve the problem. Look out for the people who are natural leaders, get them into positions of power – and do it quickly. Jump over others to get them if you have to. Don't worry about the fact they're four management layers down. Take a risk. The effect of good leadership on an organization is amazing.

Executive Timeline Gerry Robinson

1965	**Matchbox Toys**
1974	**Lex (Transport) Group**
1980	**Grand Metropolitan**
	Finance Director – Coca-Cola
	Converted Coca-Cola UK from £7m loss to £17m profit in two years.
1983	**Coca-Cola**
	Managing Director
1987	Led management buyout of Compass (the leading food service company) from Grand Metropolitan.
1991	**Granada Group**
	Chief Executive
1996	Masterminded Forte Hotel takeover.
2000	Merger of Granada Group and Compass Group.
2002–present	**Allied Domecq**
	Non-executive Chairman
2003–2004	Presenter of business series, *I'll Show Them Who's Boss* (BBC TV).
2004	Knighted in the New Year's Honours List.

There is no substitute for experience – learn more from the best minds in business

Did you know that Fifty Lessons has created a must-have digital library containing more than 350 *filmed* business lessons that can be viewed online, from home or in your office?

Through Fifty Lessons you can:

- Experience first-hand the real-life learning of some of the most influential business leaders of our time.
- Gain access to a vast array of concise lessons covering over thirty-five key leadership and management topics.
- Benefit from decades of hard-won learning and experience.

To subscribe to Fifty Lessons, and to take advantage of our special reader discount, please visit www.fiftylessons.com/readeroffer for details.

We also offer customized solutions for larger organizations, from providing lessons on DVD and print to distributing tailored lesson packages via email and corporate intranets. For further information please visit www.fiftylessons.com or

For corporate sales enquiries please contact:

BBC Worldwide Learning
Woodlands
80 Wood Lane
London
W12 oTT
United Kingdom
Tel: +44 (0)20 8433 1641
Fax: +44 (0)20 8433 2916
Email:
corporate.sales @bbc.co.uk

For any other enquiries please contact:

Fifty Lessons
Fitzroy House
11 Chenies Street
London
WC1E 7EY
United Kingdom
Tel: +44 (0)20 7636 4777
Fax: +44 (0)20 7636 4888
Email:
info@fiftylessons.com